Living the Reiki Precepts:

embracing the Reiki Principles in everyday life

by

Keziah Gibbons

Living the Reiki Precepts: embracing the Reiki principles in everyday life

© Keziah Gibbons 2014

Published by LALaS, Lincoln UK

ISBN978-1-910148-08-2

Cover image by Yuko Dodds and Keziah Gibbons

Translations by Maria Mainitz

for Lili

You bring your own colours; in you music turns to dance,

Your learning is a teaching; you bring the real to true.

May you be blessed by all that is and all that is be blessed by you.

Love, from Mum

Acknowledgements

I thank my guides; those I am aware of, and those whom I have not seen but I know are with me.

My gratitude and respect to the three people who have formally taught me Reiki. In chronological order:

Marion Saraswati Muentefer, a being who radiates love and gentle power from the very depths of her being. Marion, it was you who first laid your hands on me in healing, and who opened me to this beautiful gift. Although it took me many years to return to the Reiki path, it was those first steps with you which allowed me a point to start from. Thank you.

John M. Greaves, a dedicated healer and teacher of Reiki, sent by Spirit. John, you supported me in my healing process as I fumbled my way back to wellness, and then when I was able you began to teach me. What you passed on to me is a great gift, a gift of peace, and I hope to honour the dedication, passion and integrity with which you taught in my practice of Reiki. I thank you.

Catherine Birkenhead, whose joy and grace flow peacefully forth, touching those she meets deeply. Cathy, you introduced me to my drum and its medicine, showed me how to begin to explore my own presence in the world of Spirit, and showed me how I could connect simply and honestly with the world of Nature. Thank you.

I would like to thank the thoughtful and peace-loving Maria Mainitz for providing the translations, essential to the creation of this book.

I would also like to acknowledge the contribution of those who have surrounded me as I wrote this book, who have been sources of nourishment and inspiration. Lili, embodiment of unfettered joyful energy, to you this book is dedicated. Janice, the Magician and the Empress, and Graham, the Rowan, who have supported me in many ways, have been teaching and sharing their own special magics as I wrote this book, and to whom I owe those NLP techniques which I have adapted for the Precepts. Each has been a model in their own way. My dad, Brian, who has supported in other ways, and who has exemplified the art of quietly observing, understanding, and speaking with authority, which I hope to emulate in the writing of this book.

G-G, who is generous and compassionate and an all-round exemplary chap. Susie, whose walk over coals has taught her to connect to the bare earth under her feet. Samuel, the Yorkshireman, whom I hope to see more of over the coming years. Steve, who has in his own discipline become a Master/Teacher, and who has been on hand to ground me with a swift reality check many a time. And Jodie, Pete, Maia and Brew, each of whom I have a lot of love for and who collectively welcomed me often and warmly to their home when I travelled to Leeds to visit my teacher.

There are many others in my life who have also shared laughter, joy, and strength and support with me. You know who you are, and to each of you I extend my gratitude and many blessings. These few paragraphs cannot express how blessed I feel for all in my life.

Keziah

November 2014

Introduction

When we first start practising Reiki, we receive a set of precepts as part of our training. Although the precepts are simple, it is not always easy to know how to live by them, or to bring them into your everyday life. Many of us are busy with career, family, and other time- and attention-consuming concerns. Some of us just do not know where or how to start bringing them into our lives. This book is intended as a tool to help practice the precepts consciously and easily. It is a set of suggestions or ideas for practices to bring the precepts into our lives and keep them there. The idea is that by practising some or all of the exercises in order to bring the precepts into our lives consciously, we will begin to incorporate them into our way of being unconsciously.

This book evolved as I underwent my own Reiki training. As well as practising my meditations, self-healing, and Reiki practice on other people, I wanted to explore the precepts in more depth. I wanted to know how I could know them, understand them, and live by them, instead of simply reciting them in the mornings as part of my daily routine. I was not a nun or a recluse, but a busy mother involved in setting up my own business. I did not want to change this, but to find ways to live more Reiki within my other life choices. This book is a result of my reflections during this process and the specific exercises which I set myself and meditations which I practised in order to try to grasp the precepts fully.

As I was writing this book I became more and more aware of how the precepts overlap with each other. Frequently, I have been unsure which precept to categorise an exercise under.

Through my experience I have reinforced my belief that everyone can live the Reiki precepts. It is not necessary to be a monk or a nun, to give up vast swathes of time for meditation and reflection, or to cancel other commitments. This book is aimed at the ordinary person who is at any stage of their Reiki journey. Some dedication, however, is important. You may find that as you practice the exercises in this book you naturally begin to make changes in your life, and in yourself, the way you handle things, and the actions which you choose to take. I hope that you will find this an enriching experience and a useful tool on your Reiki path.

You can use this book in a number of ways. You could work through the exercises one by one, or you could choose those which resonate the most with your being and your lifestyle. You could choose a precept which you would like to work on and work through all the exercises in that chapter. You could use the different interpretations and ideas within the book as a springboard for your own reflection about the precepts and their role in your own life. Each chapter contains suggestions to help you to practice the precepts within yourself and in your interactions with you environment. I have also created at least one meditation for each precept, which you are free to repeat just as often as you would like to.

I share this book, not as an instructional manual from someone who has all the answers, but as an offering from peer to peer, in the hope that the exercises contained within will be as useful for you as they have been for me. I wish that you will be able to use this book to actively deepen your Reiki experience.

I hope that you will enjoy the book, just as you will find it to be a useful tool for growth. Whoever you are and wherever your Reiki path takes you, I wish you all the best for your journey.

Reiki blessings,

Keziah

Contents

What is Reiki and Why Should I be Living the Reiki Precepts?

Rei-Ki: Universal Life Force-Energy. This is the essence of Reiki, and it's what we work with when we 'do' Reiki in any way.

Reiki is passed on from teacher to student by an in-person ritual ceremony which opens the student to the Reiki energy, allowing them to become a channel for Reiki, and to use it for healing. A practitioner of Reiki learns to allow the Reiki energy to flow through them.

Healing is a fundamental part of Reiki, being both an effect and a purpose. Channelling or receiving Reiki energy helps to stimulate a person's natural healing ability, sometimes having spectacular results and resolving long-term issues, sometimes more gently simply improving a person's experience. Healing is what Reiki does. And so the Reiki practitioner needs to be consciously working on healing themselves and others to truly embody the Reiki practice.

The Reiki precepts can be seen as a theoretical part of Reiki where the channelling of energy is the practice. And of course the practice of the precepts is a part of Reiki in itself. When practicing the Reiki precepts, we not only improve the experience of life for ourselves and those around us – an important effect in itself – but we by default become more strongly connected to the Reiki, the Universal Life Force Energy, which we live out through the precepts. We become ourselves an expression of Reiki.

The Precepts in Different Translations

The Reiki precepts come to us from a document written by Mikao Usui; one of few which express his teachings in written form. The precepts, like all of the teachings, originated in Usui Sensei's native language of Japanese. If you don't speak Japanese, you will be relying on a translation. Over the years, in different lineages and with different translators, and indeed with translations into several languages, some quite different versions of the precepts have arisen. But don't worry. Even if one translation was accepted as true throughout the Reiki world, there would still be different interpretations on them, and part of your job as a Reiki practitioner is to interpret the precepts in a manner which is appropriate and applicable to you, now. Like the channelling of Reiki itself, you need only still yourself and focus, and the correct understanding will flow through you.

The Reiki precepts in Japanese are:

招福の秘法
萬病の靈薬

今日丈けは　怒るな
心配すな　感謝して
業をはげめ　人に親切に
朝夕合掌して心に念じ
口に唱えよ

心身改善
臼井靈気療法

肇祖　臼井甕男

Transliteration/pronunciation:

Shōfuku no hihō
manbyō no reiyaku

kyō dake wa
okoruna
shinpaisuna
kanshashite
gyō wo hakeme
hito ni shinsetsu ni
asayū gasshōshite kokoro ni nenji
kuchi ni tonaeyo

shinshin kaizen
Usui Reiki Ryōhō

chōso

Usui Mikao

The version of the precepts which I use is thus:

The secret prayer of inviting happiness
The miracle medicine against all illness

today only
do not get angry
do not worry
be grateful
work hard/diligently
be kind towards people
Every morning and evening fold your hands together and pray/recite from your heart
chant from your mouth

mind and body
betterment/improvement
Usui Reiki Ryōhō (name of organisation, literally translated Usui Reiki Treatment)

Originator

Usui Mikao
Japanese version courtesy of Yuko Dodds, transliteration and translation courtesy of Maria Mainitz.

But different versions of the precepts are around, and in the sections at the beginning of each chapter I will try to cover the different translations and their interpretations. The great thing about any set of precepts is that their power lies in the way in which you, the practitioner, apply them. You are a unique individual and the circumstances in which you live are unique to you. You will know when a certain application of a precept is right for you.

Kyo dake wa

Today Only - Just for Today - At Least for Today

Interpretations

'Just for Today' is sometimes regarded as a prelude to the precepts, coming before them but not as part of them. Sometimes it is even included as the beginning of each phrase which contains a precept. The Reiki precepts were not written and passed on without a great deal of thought, and for this reason we must regard 'Just for Today' as an important part of the precepts, and indeed I believe that the other precepts are each an expression of this fundamental base. We can interpret it either as a part of each precept or as a separate precept of its own. Deeper reflection on the meaning of this simple phrase can help us to create an attitude which informs not only our approach to the precepts, but our approach to every aspect of life.

One concept which fits well with the 'Just for Today' principle is that of mindfulness. Mindfulness is a useful concept, and I do not know of anybody who practices mindfulness techniques who has not found it to be of enormous benefit to them. By mindfulness, I mean both the cultivation of mindfulness practice through meditation, and the application of this practice in daily life. When we live mindfully, we live 'in the moment' – or, to put it another way, 'just for today'.

Another message which 'Just for Today' conveys to us is to take one day at a time. Many of our goals can seem huge, when we think of all the things that we have to do to reach that goal or how long we may have to do it for. So instead of saying 'I will follow the Reiki precepts forever', something which may seem an impossible task, we can say 'I will follow the Reiki precepts today' and let tomorrow take care of itself. Soon we will start to realise that by using this approach we managed to follow the Reiki precepts yesterday, and the day before, and today are practising them with ease.

A third interpretation of 'Just for Today' is the reminder to concentrate on what we are doing today. Sometimes we can get so tangled up in grand plans, or so overwhelmed, that we forget to be aware of today. If we can wake up in the mornings and ask ourselves, 'What am I doing today? Why am I doing it?' we can start to regain a sense of perspective on our world, on what is important and what is not so important. If we concentrate on fulfilling today's purpose to the best of our ability, and being aware wholly of what we are doing and why we are doing it, we may find that our lives and minds become clearer and easier.

Exercises

☼ Take time out to meditate – today, or every day. Sit up straight or lie down. The important things in meditation are that you are comfortable, but awake. Some people like to keep a straight spine so that energy can flow unimpeded between the chakras, but you should be comfortable. It is best to meditate, especially at first, in a quiet, clean and pleasant place where you cannot be disturbed – if you have a Reiki room or space this is ideal - but as you become more practiced you will begin to find that you are able to access this clear state of mind anywhere.

Being in This Moment Meditation

Take your time to get into a comfortable posture. If you are sitting up, try to put the weight on your sit bones, and hold your shoulders above your hips. Rest your hands in your lap or by your sides, so that your arms and shoulders are supported. Let the crown of your head be the highest point on your body. I am sure that you know how best to seat yourself comfortably.

Now that you are comfortable, notice your breathing. Take the time to exhale fully. Expel all of the air from your lungs, starting at the stomach, pushing it out through the chest, throat, nose and mouth. Exhale until you are completely empty and any stale air has been chased out of your lungs. Now follow your body's impulse and breathe in. You can pull some Reiki in with your breath if you feel that it would help you to be relaxed and fully present in the moment. Now follow this rhythm for a short time, expelling all of the air with your exhale, and inhaling fully, feeling the life force fill your lungs with each new breath in, letting it seep through your body as you breathe out.

You may notice some thoughts running busily through your mind. This is completely normal, and if you do notice them at any time during the meditation, just be aware of them, and return your attention to your breathing and your awareness of the moment. The thoughts are part of the moment, but they are not the main or the only part, so you can easily take your focus away from them.

As you exhale any stale air, and inhale the life energy, just become aware of those parts of your body which are supported by your seat. You may feel a sensation of weight, or of heaviness where parts of your body touch the chair or the ground. Take a moment to notice what this feels like. Suspend any judgement, and just notice how your body feels.

Now expand your awareness to the rest of your body. How do those parts of you which are in contact with the air feel? What is happening on the inside? You may feel certain sensations within you, may be aware of your body's weight, temperature, shape, and the delightful way in which your body supports you. Just be aware of this, as you breathe slowly in and out.

As you notice your body's feel in space, start to tune in to your other senses, and notice, without judgement, what your senses tell you. Maybe your eyes are closed or open, and you can notice the different qualities of light and darkness which come in through your eyes. Notice whether there is any colour within your field of vision, and if you can see any shapes. Be aware of any thoughts you may have about the objects that you see, but let those thoughts flow past as you focus on experiencing the sense of just being here, now.

Now bring your focus in to notice if there are any smells coming in. Notice whether smells bring thoughts or reactions with them, but just experience that. Try to suspend judgement – experience the smells without any labels such as good or bad. Now notice whether your mouth tastes of anything – or of nothing – and notice what that brings.

You may be noticing sounds which are close by, or more distant. Notice the quality of these sounds, the volume, the pitch, whether they are constant or intermittent. Allow the sounds to pass you by without judgement, without meaning. This is your time and you can experience the sounds of the world around you as you are here, now, without reaction; without impulse.

As you notice the feel, sights, smells and sounds around you, bring your awareness back to your breathing. Notice the way that life energy is moving into you with every inhale, and any stale energy is being expelled as you exhale. Take the time to notice what this feels like. Expand your awareness now to be aware of your entire body, as you start to come out of this meditation, and to notice whether you would like to allow yourself some movements. You might want to start with the fingers, the toes, the ankles and wrists, just giving them a little wiggle or a shake, allowing movement to return to you. If your eyes have been closed you might want to open them, and you might want to sit up or shift your weight in your seat, maybe allow yourself a delicious, sensual, stretch. Take your time to come back, and when you are ready, you can let yourself have a little smile, fully aware of what it's like to be you, here, in this moment.

☼ Vow to spend just today following the Reiki precepts. Write them down and place them somewhere in the space where you will spend your time today – on your desk, on a wall in your studio, in your kitchen or living room, in your car, in your coat pocket or even on the back of your hand. Every time you notice them check that what you are doing today is in line with the precepts. Try to keep them in mind with every decision made, word spoken and action taken today so you can really bring them into your life.

☼ Send Reiki to your day, or to any special or routine event that you've got planned for today. By using Reiki we connect both to the moment in which we are living, and to the recipient or target of our Reiki. So by sending Reiki to your day you are forming a strong and special connection to today.

✿ When you wake up in the morning, take a moment to be really consciously aware of what you are doing today. Is there a particular task which you want to accomplish? Why is it important? Who will you be spending your time with? What do you need from them, and what can you give to them? Where will you be? Is this the best environment? When you ask yourself these questions, you accomplish two things: you check that you are spending today in the best way which you possibly can, and you prime yourself to always focus on the task at hand, and not to let your thoughts drift off.

✿ An exercise involving relationships and just for today is to follow a relationship instinctively and without fear. This means that with each person you meet, pay attention to the current encounter and only the current encounter. You could forget about any past dealings you may have had with this person, and act as if you would never see that person again. By letting go of the past and future as you deal with other people you will become fully present in all of your relationships, and will learn where to best give your energies.

✿ Examine the purpose of each action and interaction. As a wise woman once said to me, *What is your intention and where is your attention?* If the two do not match, then you are not living fully in today, and you are wasting both. Your attention and intention should always be matched. For example, if your intention is to treat someone with Reiki but your attention is on what you will be having for lunch when you've finished, you are not getting the best out of yourself.

Your recipient may still receive the Reiki, but will not receive the really powerful force of focussed intent; in the meantime, you are still giving the treatment, and thinking about your lunch has not stopped your hunger. Ask yourself this question whenever you can, whenever you start a task or are halfway through. If you don't find it easy to redirect your thoughts in this way, schedule time to look back over the day's actions and interactions and examine them in this manner. With practice you will form the mental habit of ensuring your own presence in each moment.

✿ Think with your feet. Take your attention down to the soles of your feet. This will ground you in the present in two ways – by removing attention from the mindless thoughts which tend to swirl around our head areas, and focussing it at the other end of your body – and also because the sensations which you will notice will be physical and unique to your surroundings, and so make you more conscious of where you are. Notice how your feet feel – are they bare or shod? What are you treading on? Or are they in the air as you rest on another part of your anatomy? Are they moving? Notice whether or when the way your feet feel changes.

✿ Examine each person you meet. Notice how they hold themselves, how they look, how they sound. Be aware of your own reactions. Sometimes this can be uncomfortable – remember, you are just observing and they are just reactions. Forget about the meaning of them and try to observe without attaching meaning. This encourages a mindfulness of response in our relationships.

☼ Take time out to take a walk in nature. What do you see, hear, feel, smell? What is it like and what is it like for you? Try to put aside everything else for this time and just be aware of the sights, sounds, feelings and smells of a place. Try coming back at different seasons. What do you notice?

☼ Think about the impact which you have on your environment. Is there anything disharmonious about the way you live? The chances are, what with all of the environmentally unsound practices which are tied in to living in today's society, the answer is yes. Can you think of something which you can change – perhaps something small, which you can do today – to start redressing this balance?

☼ Take a moment to define your attitude to the world around you. How do you feel? What is right? What is wrong? Is there anything which you would like to see/do/experience differently? What do you need to be able to do that? How can you find those resources? Can you do it today? Now?

☼ Take some moments each morning to set your intention for today. What do you wish to achieve with these precious hours? What is your purpose today? You could do this as a meditation or as an intention to which you send Reiki. You could draw it or write it, represent it as a sound or a movement. If at any point in your day you feel lost, return to your picture/word/sound/movement. Remember what you are here for today.

Okolu-na

Do not anger - I will not be angry – Do not rise to anger

Interpretations

This particular precept does not seem to have much variance in translation, and at first glance appears to be forbidding something rather than providing guidance in a positive way. However by looking at the situations in which anger arises, and thinking consciously about how we could behave instead, we learn to take responsibility for our own emotional state. This responsibility and ownership of our own state of being is the great gift of this particular precept.

So how do we go about not angering? It seems a pretty tall order. One way in which we can do so is to recognise and take hold of our tempers when anger does start to arise, and using this recognition to take control of ourselves. Over time we will start to claim our states before anger takes it out of our control.

Another way to interpret the instruction not to anger is to focus on general well-being before angry situations arise. So we could cultivate a normal state of calm, serenity, joy, or any other positive state which we might like to have instead of anger.

One feeling which is often construed as anger, and which I believe is covered by the precept, is that of frustration. The anger comes when we allow our frustration at things not being as we believe they should be to get the better of us. One way to prevent this is to practice mindful acceptance of the world as it is, and not compare it to a mental ideal which reality can never equal. We must teach ourselves patience and practice mindfulness as we can.

Oftentimes when we are angry we feel that we are angry *at* something. Someone or something has *made us* angry. This may be the case, and what someone else says or does may be beyond our control. But we can make small changes now in the way that we perceive that situation, so that it is no longer a cause of anger but simply a situation.

These are ways to deal with unnecessary anger, and sometimes situations arise in which a feeling of anger is righteous. In these situations righteous anger is generally a tool to protect oneself or others, and to stop harm from happening. If such an unfair or harmful situation causes us anger, we can own the emotion and use it to try to think of more constructive ways in which to prevent the damage or unfairness which is happening. Basically, if anger is telling you that something has to be changed, you can acknowledge that necessity, thank the anger for bringing it to your attention, and then let go of the anger and calmly and steadily go about making that change in the most constructive way possible.

Sometimes we can be angry because we or someone we love have been hurt. We may nurture anger, at ourselves and at other people, for years because of some hurt. However real that injury is or was, by guarding anger at the person who hurt us, we are only harming ourselves. There is a real power in learning to forgive, to let go, and to embrace the new, and that power is part of the power of the precept.

Now that we have explored some different forms of anger and practices which can help us to meet the demands of this precept, here are some specific exercises to practice:

Exercises

⚙ Try to notice over the next few days every time you get angry, frustrated, or in any other such negative reactive state. As you recognise that anger is arising, stop, feel the ground under your feet, and take a deep breath, sending your awareness down as you do so. Keep breathing like this for as long as is necessary, feeling the angry feelings drain away into the ground, and the steady, reassuring presence of the earth supporting you and sending you benign energy.

✪ As you breathe your anger out, ask yourself, 'what was I angry about?' If the answer is that reality has not lived up to how you had imagined it, you can let go of the anger. Stop and look at your reality without expectations, without judgement, and feel the anger become replaced by a calm acceptance. This is just the way things are right now.

✪ Stop, and make a list of the things which anger you. Now examine each one in turn. Ask yourself, 'what is the purpose of the anger?' Try to think about how you might handle the situation without anger. You may need to realise that the situation is not important to you, and concentrate your attention on something which will make you happy instead. Or there may be something real which needs changing. Write down each step which you can take to make the changes – in your internal outlook or in the outside world – which will help you to resolve the situation without anger.

✪ Sometimes people can be really frustrating. Often the people closest to us can know how to push our buttons the most. Did you know that you can intercept that feeling between your perception and your reaction? If there is something which somebody does or says which really gets you fuming, take a moment to imagine that situation now. How is it? What can you see? Is there something they are saying to you? How does it feel? The chances are that you will have an image of that annoying behaviour. Notice where you perceive that image to be in space. Can you step away from it? Drain the colour? Push it away from you? Do you hear a voice with that annoyance? Listen to it now, and hear it getting quieter. Imagine what it would be like if you could change the tone of the voice, so that it is at the opposite end of the scale from the original voice. Is the voice coming from somewhere in your head? Move it out, push it away from you. What about the feelings which you feel when you start to anger? Can you breathe into them? Where are they in your body? What if you pushed them outside of your body? Hopefully, this will make you feel better. Imagine the next time that person does that annoying behaviour. Can you see that the image is far away, drained and small? Can you hear that the voice is different, a long way away and quieter? Notice whether the angry feeling is gone. Hopefully, you will be able to use this technique, on a conscious or unconscious level, the next time you encounter that annoying behaviour. And you may find that it no longer angers or annoys you!

✿ Think of a situation where it feels like another person angers you. What are they doing or saying that winds you up so much? Imagine yourself and that other person now, here in front of you. What is happening? Note your own and the other person's body language, words, facial expressions. Step into the image now, and into the space which the other person occupies. Take on their body language, facial expressions, utter their words. What do they need? Do you think that it is their intention to provoke an anger response in you? What happens to them as you anger? Now step out of that other person, and out of the picture again. Is there another strategy which you could employ instead of anger? Picture yourself responding with a different response. Watch the you in the picture, watch the body language, watch what happens. Is it better? Now step back into the picture, into the you who is responding with something other than anger. How does it feel? What are the resources that you have drawn on? Is there anything else you need? Step back out of the picture and give yourself any other resources that the you in the picture might need. Now imagine a time, sometime in the future, maybe the next time that you find yourself in such a situation. Can you see yourself doing things differently, listening intelligently and responding resourcefully and without anger? It's good, isn't it?

☼ Next time you begin to feel angry, stop and breathe. Notice your anger, how it feels, where it started. What specifically caused you to anger? Could you have responded differently? What thoughts are going through your head? Take each thought, and ask yourself, 'what is going on here? Have I understood the situation? Is there any other explanation?' Keep asking yourself these questions about every thought, until you understand in minute detail what has caused the anger. Remember that it's OK to change your mind, to let go of any unhelpful beliefs. Often our emotional reactions are based on faulty reasoning, and it only takes a little examination to realise that there is nothing to be angry about.

⚙ If something is repeatedly obstructing your sense of calm, take time to look at the situation as a whole. Is there a boundary that you need to set? Often we will get angry or frustrated because we feel that our boundaries and limits have not been respected. Setting aside these feelings, define the boundary clearly in words. Explain it to yourself. Now think about who else might need to know about this boundary's existence. Regardless of whether you think that they should already know or not, take the time to communicate it to them clearly and calmly. Every time the boundary is pushed or crossed, re-iterate it with calm. You have a right to have your boundaries respected and a responsibility to communicate those boundaries, just as others have a right to have their own boundaries respected. If someone understands yet repeatedly violates your boundaries, remove yourself from the situation. Practicing an angerless state does not mean putting up with unacceptable behaviour.

⚙ Practice your calm exterior. Think about what it means to be calm. Notice your breathing, the way you hold yourself. Your muscles may be relaxed and you may have a little smile, or other serene expression, on your face. Practice this physiology whenever you can, and if you feel anger begin to arise, fake the calm. Make your face, body, breathing, express calm, so that nobody can tell that you are not completely calm. As you practice creating a state of calm, you may find that your true state follows naturally.

⚙ If your anger serves a purpose, such as that of protecting yourself or others, inspect it. You will find that within your state of righteous anger are many other resources, which may include strength, determination, sense of justice, and motivation. Harness these resourceful states, and use them to make a difference to the situation at hand. And try doing this with a clear, calm head. It is by harnessing the useful resources attached to such emotions, whilst refusing the unhelpful emotions themselves, that people make a true difference to the world.

✪ Sometimes anger is a consequence of not being at peace with reality. The best way to avoid this is to practice mindfulness, and this is not always easy. One technique for disassociating enough to see and accept reality as it really is, is to imagine that you are telling or writing a story, with yourself as a character in it. If you can, see the letters on the page, and imagine yourself reading about what is happening. As you read, see only the words, see that they are printed on the page in ink, and know that whatever is happening to the character already is. You don't have to react to it. Read the story without judgements or attachment, as if the characters and plot are new to you and you have yet to judge, and you may find that you become more at peace with reality.

✪ Plant or obtain a plant for your home, work, or any place where you spend a lot of time. Remember that as we breathe in oxygen and breath out carbon dioxide, so the plant breathes in carbon dioxide and breathes out oxygen. If you feel anger arising, breathe it out as carbon dioxide, and know that the plant will breathe it in as life. Then breathe in the oxygen which the plant has made for you, feeling the pleasure of reciprocal life, and knowing that your anger has been turned by the plant into something vital and beautiful. It's important to remember as you breathe out your anger that the plant will ingest it as something nourishing. This both allows you to change your focus to well-wishing another living being, and ensures that the plant receives cleansed energy from you.

☼ If you find that it is less easy to be calm in a certain place, for example, at work or even in a certain room in the house, look at your environment. See if there are changes which you can make so that it becomes a calm place to be. This may include getting rid of clutter, ensuring that you have a comfortable space to sit and be, playing calming or relaxing music, even changing the colour-scheme if it makes you uncomfortable. Add a few pictures of things, people, or places which make you feel calm and practice breathing deeply for a few breaths every time you enter that space, so that it becomes a place of calm for you.

☼ If you find yourself getting angry at any point, place your hands over your forehead above each eyebrow. By doing so you draw bloodflow away from that part of your brain which harbours reactive anger, as well as the fight or flight response, and back into your logical forebrain. At the same time breathe, and if you would like to draw some Reiki into yourself, this is also a good thing to do as it has a calming effect.

☼ Meditate to ground yourself. This meditation is best done sitting, lying, or standing with bare feet on the earth, and will also work indoors or with sturdy footwear if weather or other practicalities do not allow this. The important thing is that you are taking time out to connect yourself to the earth, so that any unhelpful feelings will automatically be drawn out of you and 'earthed', like in electricity:

Earthing meditation

Get comfortable in the place where you are going to do your meditation. As you place yourself on the ground, you can notice how it feels underneath you, notice how your weight settles comfortably down into the ground and the surface area that this takes up. Now take a moment to become really aware of your breathing. You don't have to slow it down any, just be aware of the easy way in which you breathe in and down into your stomach, and then breathe out, and with each out-breath, notice yourself settling into the ground. So you're breathing in, down into your tummy, and as you breath out, letting go, allowing the earth to support you, to take your weight underneath you. And now as you breathe in, I'd like you to continue to breathe deeply into your stomach, and as you breathe out, just imagine that breath is travelling steadily down your body, to the earth. That's good.

And as you continue to breathe, you can notice whether as that deep breathing, as it travels down to the earth, is able to permeate the earth a little bit, so that you are now breathing down into the earth. And as you do so, you may notice sensations where your breath and your body meet the earth, and the earth reaches for you as you sink into it.

As you continue to breathe deeply, allowing that breath to reach down into the earth, you can start to imagine that you are sending out roots, into the earth. If you're not touching the earth directly, be aware that the earth's energy field reaches you anyway – she's big, and earth energy is strong. And each time you breathe out, your roots may begin to extend further, and deeper into the earth. That's good.

And as you breathe out, letting any sensations which you're not completely comfortable with follow your breath down into the earth, to be broken up for nutrients, you may notice that as you breathe in, you are able to pull some nourishment from the earth's depths into your roots. Notice any sensations in your roots, and in the places where your body is supported by the earth, and notice whether you can feel the earth's nourishing, supporting, grounding force seeping into you. We are all inside the earth's magnetic field, and she pulls us all to her, centred. And it's a wonderful thing.

And now, you can just stay here for as long as you like, and really notice the sensations of your body on the earth, your roots extending down, any toxins draining away from you, and the goodness of nourishment as it enters you from the earth, as you continue to breathe deeply.

And now, as you visualise yourself planted in the earth, you can be aware of your hidden depths, of the fact that as you are on this world, you are always connected with the earth. And you can be aware of the possibilities which this gives you for expansion, for growth, as you relax.

And now, continuing to breathe in and out deeply, you can bring your attention back to where your roots extend down into the earth, and, from your very centre, send down a sensation of gratitude into your roots. Gratitude, to the earth, which supports and nourishes you, allowing you room to grow, and to yourself, for giving yourself this time, this connection, and this nourishment.

And now bring your attention away from your roots, knowing they will always be there any time that you need to connect to the earth, and bring your attention back to those parts of your physical body which are in contact with the earth. Notice again, your weight on them, and notice how those parts of your body support the rest of your body which rests on top of them. As you breathe into your tummy, bring your awareness upwards, and notice your feet, legs, buttocks, hips. Become aware of your stomach as you breathe into it, and notice that the breath also rises into your chest, your shoulders. And as you start to think about coming round, you may want to wiggle your fingers a little, just to regain an awareness of your body. And now, as your focus returns naturally to your head, you may want to roll it gently towards one shoulder, and then the other, or to bow your chin to your chest, and then up, and maybe lengthen your spine, as you become aware of your whole body again.

And now, with a little wiggle in the fingers and toes, you may want to shift position, or to stretch a certain part of your body, and when you are ready, you can open your eyes and be present once more in your surroundings.

☼ Sometimes we retain old or fresh anger because someone has done something to us, or we can be angry at ourselves for something we feel we've done wrong. The thing we are angry about may be a big thing, or a little thing, and it may not always be easy to consider forgiveness. By holding onto the anger, and not forgiving another person or ourselves, however, we are preventing ourselves from healing, from moving on. Forgiveness is not about absolving responsibility, but about releasing ourselves from the shackles of anger which a particular incident might have left us with.

The first thing we need to do in order to forgive, is to decide what it is that we need to forgive. You might already know what it is that needs to be forgiven, and you may be unsure or think that it is silly. It's OK. Even if one part of our brains says that it's silly to need to forgive a certain thing, there's another part of our brain that needs to anyway, and it is this part of the brain that we're dealing with today. So take a moment and decide who you need to forgive, whether it is yourself or another person, and what you are forgiving them for.

Now picture that person, doing the thing that needs to be forgiven, really clearly. You may just see them, or you may notice sounds, smells, even feelings. That's OK. Take that scene and shrink it down into a little imaginary box in front of you. Shrink it so much that the box fits into the palm of your hand.

Now put your hands around the little box with the scene inside. You will send Reiki to the scene, and to the person. Take a moment to centre yourself and connect to Reiki in whatever way you normally do. If you know the symbol for distant healing, you can use this now, and this technique will also be effective without it. Send Reiki into the box. Send it to the incident which you are forgiving, and to the person whom you are forgiving. If you wish, you can affirm aloud, to yourself or to the person in the box, that you are forgiving them, and releasing them. Tell them that you wish them only healing for their highest good. Continue to send the Reiki for as long as you need to and then disconnect as you normally would, making sure to allow the box to disappear as you disconnect from the energy.

This is a powerful technique because Reiki only allows you to send healing and good wishes, and you cannot do Reiki and be angry at the same time. It helps to heal you, heal the effects of the incident, and also the person whom you are forgiving, so that they may be enabled to move out of any destructive behaviours.

You can use this technique for anything which you feel you need to forgive. If it is something large or serious, or distressing for any reason, only hold the scene for as long as you feel able. You can always come back to it if you feel that it does not work first time or that you are not ready to forgive. The power of this technique, however, does then allow you to regain control of your own life, without anger.

Shinpai suna

Do not worry - I will not worry – do not succumb to worry

Interpretations

As with the previous precept, the edict not to worry can seem like a bit of a tall order. And again, it really is just an instruction to start to govern your own state of mind and of being.

One of the best ways to do this is to practice mindfulness. This book is not, and does not pretend to be, a guide to mindfulness practice, and you may find that you want to research this topic separately. One practice that does seem to eliminate the tendency to worry, along with bringing greater mindfulness, is regular meditation, and I recommend that you consider this if you do not practice already.

Another really useful method to remain calm and worry-free is to concentrate on your breathing, just being aware of yourself here now, so that you are present in the moment. Presence in the moment is a wonderful way to eliminate worry, as worries are inevitably a product of your mind focussing on something else, in the future, or in another place, or more likely than not something that will never come to pass anyway. No wonder it doesn't feel right! If you are truly present in the moment, you will find that you are not able to worry in this way about these hypothetical situations.

Another way to eliminate worries, is, in short, to get your priorities right. When you really focus on what is important, you can realise that the other things which you worry about are just your mind, latching on to things. Imagine what it would be like if your mind was able to leave those things alone and be calm. How does it feel? Wonderful? Perhaps a bit daunting, all that space for your mind?

Some worries are real, and some are less so. Sometimes the things that you worry about do require action, yet more often than not it is just your mind's way of occupying you, steering you away from the present moment in which you reside. Worry is simply the repeated turning over of a problem in your mind, and if this is not useful the first time, it may not be so the fifty-second, or thousandth time either.

There is an old and oft-repeated piece of wisdom which seems particularly appropriate here. That is:

May I be granted the strength to change the things I can, the grace to accept the things I cannot, and the wisdom to know the difference.

This combination of strength, grace and wisdom seem like an ideal to aim for in following this particular precept.

Exercises

☼ At a moment in which something is really worrying you, and you need to get it out of your mind, take a moment to bring yourself back to the here and now. Start by acknowledging yourself, being wherever you are, doing whatever you are doing, and worrying. Acknowledge the worry, don't try to pretend it's not there. Then, having acknowledged this, take a moment to focus your attention elsewhere. Notice your breathing. Notice if it is deep or shallow, rapid or slow. Is it comfortable breathing? Can you make it more comfortable? Keep noticing your breathing as you take a moment to become really aware of your posture. Is it comfortable? Can you make yourself more comfortable? Keep noticing your breathing. Now look around you, listen to the sounds, feel any sensations which you might have. Are you smelling anything? Do you have a taste in your mouth? Notice your surroundings as you continue to breathe. You may notice at this stage that the worry has left you, or is getting smaller, further away, and more insignificant. Continue to focus on your breathing, posture and surroundings for as long as you need.

✿ If you still find yourself worrying, take a moment to ask yourself, 'what is the purpose of this worry?' Everything which your mind does has a higher purpose, and is a result of your brain trying to process information, act appropriately, and, ultimately, protect you from harm. Ask yourself what the worry hopes to achieve. When you have found out what the purpose of the worry is, thank yourself for having your own best interests at heart, and ask yourself if there is any other way of achieving this purpose? You might surprise yourself with what you come up with.

✿ Just for fun, a few questions to ask yourself if you find yourself worrying

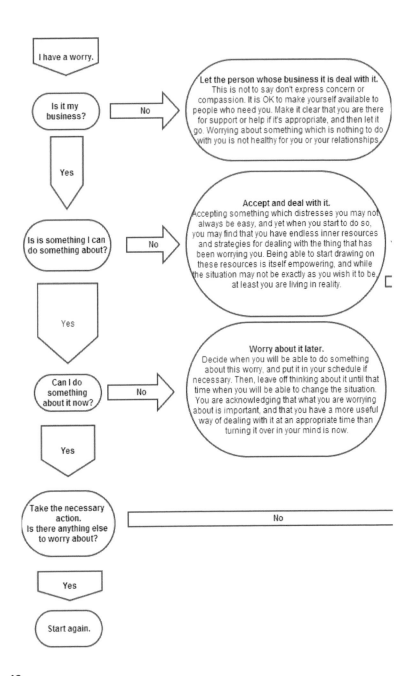

I have a worry.

Is it my business?

No → **Let the person whose business it is deal with it.** This is not to say don't express concern or compassion. It is OK to make yourself available to people who need you. Make it clear that you are there for support or help if it's appropriate, and then let it go. Worrying about something which is nothing to do with you is not healthy for you or your relationships.

Yes

Is is something I can do something about?

No → **Accept and deal with it.** Accepting something which distresses you may not always be easy, and yet when you start to do so, you may find that you have endless inner resources and strategies for dealing with the thing that has been worrying you. Being able to start drawing on these resources is itself empowering, and while the situation may not be exactly as you wish it to be, at least you are living in reality.

Yes

Can I do something about it now?

No → **Worry about it later.** Decide when you will be able to do something about this worry, and put it in your schedule if necessary. Then, leave off thinking about it until that time when you will be able to change the situation. You are acknowledging that what you are worrying about is important, and that you have a more useful way of dealing with it at an appropriate time than turning it over in your mind is now.

Yes

Take the necessary action. Is there anything else to worry about?

No

Yes

Start again.

42

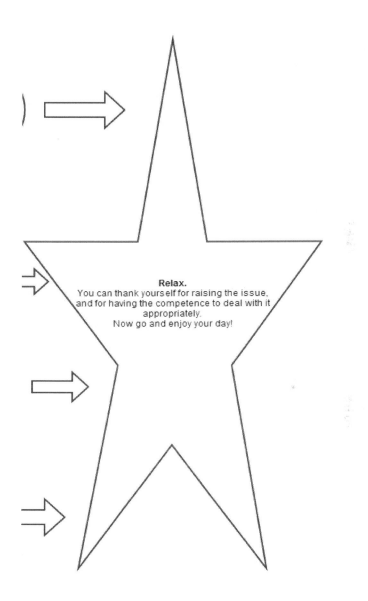

Relax.
You can thank yourself for raising the issue,
and for having the competence to deal with it
appropriately.
Now go and enjoy your day!

43

✧ You can meditate regularly to help yourself to live more in the moment and worry free. Sit, lie down or otherwise rest somewhere comfortable where you won't be disturbed. Some people find that sitting upright on the ground or a seat is the best position for meditation:

Connecting with yourself meditation

Get yourself really comfortable somewhere that you feel safe. The next few minutes will be for you, and you can allow yourself to be really present with yourself. As you rest in the position you have chosen to best support your meditative practice, notice the ground or chair which supports you. That's great. Feel its solidity underneath you, allowing you to rest your weight down into the ground. Notice the pressure where your skin and muscles are in contact with your seat. Now draw your gaze inwards, becoming really aware of your centre, that spot inside you just behind and below your belly button where you carry all of your vital forces. You may wish to close your eyes as you do this. Now, with your attention resting on the centre of your body, the centre of your being, slowly become aware of your breathing. You may notice that as you breathe in, you are bringing energy in and down to this centre of your being. You can enjoy that. Just breathe, softly, into your centre, allowing your tummy to rise and fall, allowing your weight to sink down into the ground.

And as you continue to be aware of your breath bringing energy slowly into your centre, you may wish to expand your awareness, so that you are aware not only of your steady breathing, and the sensations that being aware of the centre of your being bring to you, and you are also aware of your torso: spine rising up your back, supported by your pelvis, ribs coming down your front, surrounding your breath nicely. As you become aware of these areas you may notice certain sensations: this means you are able to relax.

And now you can expand your attention down to your legs, and to those parts of you which are in contact with whatever is supporting you. And you may notice that these parts, so well supported, are able to relax, to soften, as you breathe.

And now you can expand your attention outwards from your torso, taking in your arms, and your shoulders. As you breathe you may notice a tendency for your muscles to soften. That's good. And lastly, you can expand your attention up, to neck, and then to your head, noticing how well it is supported, and how as you breathe in through your nose, the breath seems to bring sensations of softness to your face and head also.

And now that you're aware of your body around your breathing, you can picture yourself, where you are, right now. Picture the way you're holding yourself, and you may notice the clothes that you're wearing, and you may be able to visualise your immediate surroundings. You may see what you're sitting on as you notice it beneath you. You may see what's in front of you, or the space around you. You can see these things without attaching any particular thought to them.

As you notice these things, retain your awareness of yourself, your centre, your breathing and your body in this place. As you continue to be aware of yourself and your surroundings, notice any sounds which you might be able to hear. Notice whether they are loud or quiet, whether they are close by or far away. Notice these things from within your centre, your self.

As you continue to hold yourself and your surroundings in your focus, notice any sensations which you are receiving from your surroundings. What is the temperature? Just be aware of these feelings as you focus on your self and your being.

Notice now if there are any smells in the room with you, or anything else about your surroundings which you are now aware of. Continue to breathe and notice the soothing sensation of that air flowing easily in and out as your lungs expand and contract.

Remaining aware of your self, if you have not already opened your eyes, you can do so now, and see your surroundings from within. Here you are. As you start to become more consciously aware of all of those sensations which you have been noticing, you may find that you want to stretch a little, shift slightly or wiggle your toes or fingers. It is OK to do so.

As you sit up and notice you're aware, you're alive, you're awake, smile for yourself and your awareness. You can take this new awareness with you as you continue about your day.

☼ There is another meditation which you can do which is specifically for releasing worries and fears. It is best to do it when you are alone at home, or somewhere where you won't be disturbed. Because of the noisy nature of this meditation, you also need to be aware that you may disturb other people if they're not expecting it, which is why it is best to wait until you are alone in a safe space.

Worry Releasing Meditation

Seat yourself, on the ground or a chair, for a moment. Focus on your worries and fears, all the negative feelings that you wish to release. Gather them into one place inside you. You may feel them there, and it may be uncomfortable. It's OK; you need to know that all your worries, fears and negativity is in one place. Intend that over the next twenty minutes you will release these worries, fears and negative feelings, so that they will no longer be inside you. You may wish to set a timer so that you know when the twenty minutes is up.

Remaining seated or standing, reach into this place where you have stored all of these feelings and begin to express these worries and fears as sound. You should take care not to use words – as these carry pre-shaped meanings to them – but just allow it all to come out as sounds, expressing with your mouth, tongue and vocal chords. You may wish to move around as you do this, and to make gestures. You will continue to release these sounds for twenty minutes. You may notice that the sounds change in nature, or they may remain the same. You may feel silly; you may feel overwhelmed, or powerful, or many feelings. It's OK. Just keep letting them come, releasing and expressing these worries and fears as sounds and gestures.

After twenty minutes is up, stop the sounds and the gestures and sit back down. Breathe deeply into the centre of your being to centre yourself. Notice where the worry and fear was before. Breathe into this space as you feel the difference. Sit for ten minutes or so, breathing and grounding yourself after your experience. You may notice that this meditation has a powerful effect on you, and can release old blockages. After ten minutes, or when you are ready, you can bring yourself out of the meditation.

✿ Did you know that you can mentally 'throw out' your worry, and replace it with something else? When a worry arises, try this exercise:

Picture the worry to yourself. Notice where you place this picture in your mind's eye, whether you are in it, whether there are any colours. Notice any sounds that go with it.

Now let go of it. Clap your hands together and wiggle your toes.

Can you think of something which you used to worry about, but which now no longer worries you? If you can, try to think of something which you know it was really silly to worry about. Picture that thing. Where is this picture in your mind's eye? Are there any sounds or sensations? Notice the placing of these.

Let go of that image. Now, you need to come back to your original picture, the picture of the thing that worried you. Can you drain the colour from it? Make it smaller? Can you turn the sound down? Shrink the sensations? Now, I want you to take this picture, breathe in and grab a hold of it, and as you breathe out, blow the picture, along with its sounds and sensations, to the same place in your mind's eye as the picture of the thing you used to worry about, which you now know is silly. Blow the picture away there, and feel the sensations leaving your body, hear the sounds disappearing.

Now let go, turn away from that space. Have another wiggle. Is there something you'd like to be thinking instead of worrying? Picture yourself thinking that. Be aware of where the picture is in your mind's eye, of any colours, how vibrant they are. Hear any sounds which you might hear when you're thinking that thing, including things you may be telling yourself; feel any sensations. Really become aware of them.

Now, do you believe that the sun rises every day? Of course you do, we all know it to be true. Picture the sun rising every day to yourself. Where do you see that in your mind's eye? What are the colours like? Are there any sounds or sensations associated with knowing this to be the case?

Now return to the picture which you have of yourself thinking the thing you'd really like to think. Where is it in relation to the sun rising every day? Can you move it a bit closer? Now, as you breathe in, again you're going to gather the picture of yourself thinking the thing which you'd like to think, and as you breathe out, you're going to blow it to the place where the sun rises every day. That's right. And as you do that, notice any sounds getting louder, any sensations feeling stronger and really like this is part of you.

Think of a situation in the future where you used to worry about the particular worry we've been working on. Can you picture yourself now, thinking the thing which you've just decided you'd rather be thinking?

Take a break now as you know that you no longer worry about that thing.

☼ If you have a particular worry which you would like to alleviate, you could send Reiki to it. Get into your normal meditation or distant Reiki position, and visualise first the thing that you are worrying about. Picture the scene, and put it in a box. Shrink it down until it is small enough to fit into one of your hands. With the other hand, draw the distant healing symbol if you know it, or if you don't, just intend that Reiki will be sent to this situation for the highest healing good of all concerned. With this intention, flood the scene with Reiki for as long as you feel is necessary.

When you've finished doing this, rub or shake off your hands, allowing the picture to fade. Now make a picture of yourself worrying about this thing. Again, place this picture in the palm of one hand and cup the other over it, sending Reiki to yourself worrying. As you do this, feel the Reiki flooding in through you, through your body and mind, right into the depths of your very being. Continue this for as long as you feel you need to.

Finish off by shaking or rubbing the energy from your hands and disconnecting as normal.

✿ Create a safe, worry-free space for yourself. Depending on your resources, this may be a room, a certain spot or seat in a room, or an outside space. Stand outside of your space and picture yourself worry-free. Notice the physiology and breathing of this worry-free you particularly. As you step into the space, adopt this physiology and breathing, and consciously decide that your worries are not allowed to enter this space. Do this several times, and repeat any time you need to leave your worries behind.

✪ Take action on worries. If there is something which worries you and you can do something about it, act. If it seems like too much to sort out all at once, break it down into steps and take one step at a time. Ask anybody you need to for help – if you don't ask, you'll never know if they would have helped. Resolve any real problems which need to be resolved so that it is easier to live worry-free.

✪ Make a worry list. This is a fantastic and really helpful technique and involves carrying a pen or pencil and a piece of paper around with you. Any time you start to notice yourself worrying about something, stop, write it on the list, and put it back in your pocket. Then carry on with what you were doing before you were worrying. If you feel that you absolutely must worry, make ten minutes a day where you can sit down and do worry about the things on your list. That way you can get on with your life for the rest of the day, and you may find that very soon you can do without the ten minutes as well!

Kansha shite

Be grateful – Be humble – Give thanks for many blessings – Honour your parents, teachers and elders – Show appreciation

Interpretations

At first glance, the manifold translations of this precept can be a bit confusing, and when we look deeper, we see that they have simply been interpreted as they have been translated, and come down to different expressions of the concept of appreciating what is offered to us in life.

The concept of humility can be particularly daunting. For some people, this means backing down, negating your own power, making yourself small. I do not believe this is what Usui taught. A wise teacher once told me that humility is more about knowing your own worth: neither estimating yourself to be more important than you are or less important. For me, I would describe this as remembering that the world does not revolve around us, or around our worldviews – something we are all prone to forget at times.

With this concept comes that of respect. In one rendering, the precept teaches us to honour parents, teachers and elders. This is always good practice, and in fact, everybody is included in this concept. We should respect the wisdom and experience that each person brings with them when they enter our lives. Sometimes it is not always easy to discern this when we meet people – a fact which is exacerbated by our tendency, as human beings, to judge –and yet when you realise or remember that every single being has experience which you can only imagine, knowledge which you have not yet gained, an outlook which you may be yet to understand, we see that everybody has something to teach us, and that we must respect each person for those things which we have yet to learn. If you like, every person we meet is a teacher, every person is our elder in some way. Our job is to recognise and respect that.

Something which necessarily follows from this realisation is the need for each person to cultivate a willingness to learn. For if we all have something to teach, we all have something – many things – to learn. Try to approach each day with a willingness to learn something new, to gain new understanding, knowledge, or skills.

Another important thread of this precept is that of gratitude: the willingness and ability to appreciate each thing as it comes, and to be grateful for its existence. This concept hinges partly on the concept of oneness – the fact that all things are connected, and the existence of anything, however far outside of you it may seem, is a co-existence with yourself. How could you be other than grateful for your own existence? Or, to put it another way, accept with appreciation each thing that is, for if it is, how could it be otherwise?

Gratitude in our daily lives is something we all practice to some degree. We are all taught to say 'thank you' when we are children, and as we grow, with the formal saying of the words, we gain a feeling of gratitude. Our instruction in this precept is simply to follow that practice: to say 'thank you' and feel it – for everything we notice; everything we experience.

Exercises

☼ Say thank you: Has there ever been a time when you have received something, but never expressed your gratitude? Think now of something which you would like to say thank you for. It could be something small and seemingly unimportant; it could be something life-changing. It could be something that happened five minutes ago or twenty years in the past. Think of one thing which you would like to say thank you for, and go and thank that person. If that person is not close to you in space, send them a card or a letter to thank them. Notice the joy that rises in you as you express your gratitude, and the smile that lights up the other person's face as they share the joy of your appreciation.

☼ Say sorry: An important part of practicing humility, of claiming our place in this world, is that of taking responsibility for our actions and their consequences. If you have done something which has caused harm, whether you intended the consequences or not, you need to say sorry. This exercise is not as easy as the last one, and you may do it when you are ready. Think of the action which you would like to apologise for, and the person who you would like to say sorry to. Now go and say sorry, or write a letter or a card. Do not try to justify your action in any way – just acknowledge that you regret it. Depending on what it is, and the disposition of the person you are saying sorry to, that person may or may not forgive you, or have already forgiven you. That is not relevant. The forgiveness is their practice; the responsibility and expression of regret are yours.

☼ Celebrate your learning, knowledge and achievements by applying them. There is no point spending your time and energy learning something if you never use it. Take a moment to take stock of the things that you already know, both in your head and deep down within you. Is there something that you know which you don't apply? Why not? Can you think of a situation in which it might be useful to apply that knowledge? Use it. A great example is Reiki – you can bring it in to any situation. Self-heal as you wait for appointments, send Reiki to situations which you are in or are about to walk into (always intending the highest good), send it to people who you see are in need of some healing or even just to everyone on the bus.

☼ Go and learn something new. Anything. Is there a skill or knowledge which you'd like to have, but don't? Why don't you learn it? By learning new things all the time we are reminded of how much we don't know, as well as the pleasure of learning. It can help us to keep a 'beginner's mind'. Go and enrol in a class or ask someone who has that skill or knowledge to teach you. Commit yourself to learning this. Enjoy the pleasure of challenging yourself and growing as you learn.

☼ Take yourself outside of your comfort zone. This is, by nature, an uncomfortable experience, and a very rewarding one. You are probably expert at one or several things. You might know everything there is to know about, have a deep interest in, feel connected with those things. Those are not the things we are focussing on here. Is there something which you have never done, could not imagine yourself doing, might never even want to do? Go and do it. For somebody who does not consider themselves to be an active person this might be taking a fitness class or training to run a marathon; for somebody who is very shy this might be standing up and making a speech in public. It doesn't have to be something world-changing; it just has to be something you would not ordinarily do. By plunging yourself into a world where you do not know the language or the customs and have everything to learn, you not only gain the gift of humility in the face of your ignorance, but also the reward of exploring depths of yourself that you did not even know existed previously.

☼ Listen mindfully to what others have to teach you. With some people, it is easy to sense that they are wise, skilled, or knowledgeable, and that we can learn from them. With others, we do not always perceive it straight away. With each person that you come into contact with today, ask yourself, 'what can this person teach me?' Some people pass on knowledge or skills as formal or informal learning; other teach you directly through experience – for example, that rude person pushing past you may be there to teach you patience, or calm assertiveness. Spend today meeting each person and situation with this question in mind. At the end of the day look at what you have learned, and at what you might want to explore further. You will likely find that you have gained a lot from the rich experiences, and there may be one or two people whom you want to spend more time with in order to learn the things which they have to teach. Use these opportunities.

☼ Keep a gratitude diary. This is a popular and successful way to cultivate gratitude within yourself. Each day, find a few minutes to sit and write down five things for which you are grateful. They could be anything from the continued existence of your loved ones to the fact that you found 50p down the back of the sofa. It doesn't matter what you are grateful for; it matters that you experience gratitude.

☼ Think of those people closest to you. This may be someone you live with, a family member, or a close friend. The chances are that you know them really well – or you think you do. Is there something this person knows, or can do, or regularly experiences, which you don't? Maybe it's what they do for a living, or their hobby. Ask them if they can teach you, or if you can share their experience. This is another great way of deepening our own selves through recognising the depths of others.

☼ Send Reiki to those people who do not have the same blessings as you. By sending love and light to those who do not have what we have – a roof, safety, clean water – we learn to appreciate our own blessings more. We also recognise that it is not through our own worthiness that we have 'earned' our blessings –it could just as easily be us without. Send healing now in gratitude, and in the hope of sharing some of your blessings with others.

☼ **Gratitude Meditation**

Get comfortable, sitting or lying with spine straight and body supported. Take a moment to just relax, and breathe. Inhale deeply into your tummy, down to the very centre of your being, and as you exhale, just allow every part of you to relax. That's right. Inhale, feel yourself filling up with peaceful, calming breath, and as you exhale, relax. You can relax your toes, your feet, your calves, knees, thighs, and pelvis as you continue to breathe. Now relax your abdomen, chest, back, all of the internal organs inside of you which are keeping you here. Take your attention to your shoulders, let them drop, relax your upper and lower arms. Relax your hands, letting them drop from your wrists, maybe supported by your lap. Come back to your shoulders, breathe into them, and let them relax even more. Relax your neck, jaw, brow, and the back and crown of your head. Bring your attention back to your breathing now as you breathe gently in and out of your centre.

Can you think of a blessing which you have in your life? Something or someone with which you feel truly blessed. Take a moment now to bring that blessing to mind. Picture it in your mind's eye; notice if there's any sound. Notice the feelings that come as you contemplate this blessing in your life. You might feel certain sensations, they might be pleasant sensations. Focus on your blessing now as you say from your very centre; 'I am grateful for this blessing'. Notice that feeling of gratitude; where it is in your body; whether it's big or small; whether it is warm.

Keep hold of this feeling of gratitude as you let that visualisation of your blessing go. Take a moment to check in with your body; your centre, your limbs, your trunk, your head and face, just checking that they remain relaxed and comfortable.

Now, can you think of a situation or person in your life which you find difficult? Bring this difficult person or situation to mind now, picturing yourself finding them difficult in your mind's eye. As you watch yourself in this difficult situation, ask yourself, 'What can I learn from this situation?' Continue to breathe as you listen for the answer from within yourself. It may come in words or other sounds, or in an image, or a feeling. Just watch what comes to mind. When you have the answer, just take it and hold it within you. Now take a moment to thank yourself for recognising this learning opportunity, and thank the universe for providing it for you. You may find that the feeling of gratitude returns; in the same place within your body; it's OK. Holding on to this gratitude now, you can let go of the difficult situation or person, knowing that you can learn what you need to from it.

And bring your attention back once more to the centre of your body. Notice your breathing. Begin to come back to the room now, as you notice what your body is resting on, how you are seated, whether there is a desire to move slightly, to shift. Notice any sounds coming in from outside yourself. If you like, you can start to wiggle your fingers and toes, and when you're ready, you can open your eyes. Thank yourself one more time, for taking the time out to do this meditation, and notice whether or not you feel better now, so that you can get up and go into the world refreshed, revitalised, and ready to accept your blessings.

☼ Sometimes we need to regain a sense of perspective on the world. You can do this meditation supine or seated, or in whatever position you find helps you to relax the best.

Universal Perspective Meditation

Stop, and breathe now as you become aware of your body. Take a moment to relax, and to drop into your body. Feel what is happening with it; notice how you are supported, what shape you are in; any sensations which seem significant. Try to experience your body as energy; feel, hear and see the energy flowing through and gathering in you.

As you become aware of your body as energy, zoom your focus out a little, to imagine yourself and the room you are in. You could make a picture, or notice a feeling of expansion. You don't have to experience this deeply – just be aware.

Now zoom out a little more. Visualise the entire building you are in – if you like you could try to see and feel the energy patterns of anybody else in the building; or it may be enough to just know that they are there. Really get a sense of the building that you are in, and where you are in relation to it.

Now, you can bring your focus out even further, to the size of the street that you are on. Notice how many buildings are on the street, how many living beings there are. Try to visualise them or grasp their energy pattern.

Now expand your focus a little more, to visualise the settlement where you are. See how much energy is there, feel all of the living beings, all of the interactions which are going on.

And from there, you can make the picture even bigger, to encompass the whole country where you are located, noting your own place on that map. See yourself as a dot on the map; notice any sensations that this brings.

Now zoom out even further, to see an image of the whole globe, and notice where you are in that image, and what else you see. How does it feel to be such a small part of the picture?

You can expand your awareness more now, so that you see our whole Solar System, the sun, all of the planets, their satellites, and try to reach for where in that picture you are.

Now you can zoom out, and just imagine our galaxy, the Milky Way. See the stars spiralling into the night, notice any sensation which you associate with this image. Can you get a sense of where you are now?

One more time, expand your awareness, and visualise the Universe, eternal, endless, ever-expanding Universe, with all of the galaxies and stars which it encompasses. How does that feel? What do you notice?

Now it's time to start to come back in, so from your image of the Universe, find that spiral galaxy of ours and just zoom into that. Reach for our solar system and bring that back into your full focus. Can you find the planet Earth? Let that fill your awareness. Locate your country on the globe, and zoom in, in to your town, to your street, to the room you are in. Bring yourself back into your body. Feel yourself resting where you are. As you notice your breathing, the shape of your limbs, notice whether you have gained a new perspective. See what this perspective is; hug it in close. You will bring it with you as you come out of your meditation. Notice any sounds which are within your awareness. If you feel like it, you can wiggle your fingers or toes, or anything else which feels like it needs a wake up. You may wish to open your eyes – do so slowly, and let your surroundings slowly come back into focus. Pull the tiny muscles at the corners of your mouth up to your ears, bring your hands together, and prepare to get up, bringing your new perspective with you.

Goo hage me

Work hard – work diligently - be honest – be honest in your work – work hard – do your work honestly – apply yourself diligently – devote yourself to your work – earn your living honestly – be honest in your dealings with other people

Interpretations

The first and simplest interpretation of this precept is the edict to be honest. This can mean being truthful, and it is true that we should not be lying to ourselves or others. Lying to ourselves is particularly harmful – for if there is something we are hiding from ourselves, don't we have the right to know about it and to act accordingly?

I think that what Usui meant in this principle, is to be honest in your state of being. This again is part of mindful living, and is about recognising and knowing ourselves and the world around us. When we are honestly being, we accept ourselves. When we are honestly being, we know and accept the world around us. When we are honestly being, we are fully present in our acts and our speech. We know who we are, what we are doing, why we are doing it. We are able to question ourselves and come up with honest answers.

The interpretation which adds the concept of work onto this precept is simply an extension of this need for an honest state of being. Maybe you work a 9 to 5, or several jobs, or maybe your work is to look after children or an elderly relative. Maybe you have decided to make Reiki your work. Whatever we are doing, it is important to be fully present and committed to it – to apply ourselves with diligence. If the mind is elsewhere, no one wins. If you find that what you had considered to be your work is not something you can be fully present and comfortable in, maybe you have a different calling. All this about work is not to say don't ever have a break – we all need time and space to be fully present in our joy and leisure time, and to rest and recuperate from our efforts.

The interpretation to be honest in your dealings with other people is once again, about your state of being. As in whatever you're doing, commit yourself fully to your interactions. Keep your mind with the person you are talking to, and listen more than you talk. This doesn't mean you have to fake anything. Just be present, evaluate your reactions before you act on them, and when you do, be honest and full about that also. It's nice to get on with people, and yet sometimes we do have to challenge people's behaviours or beliefs, so when you do that, do it from a fully committed point of view as well.

Exercises

☼ **Path finding meditation – creative visualisation**

To prepare for this meditation, sit in a comfortable, upright position, in a chair or on the ground. Align your head over your spine, which rises from your hips, which sit directly underneath your shoulders. Close your eyes and take a deep breath in to your centre, centring your self, and notice how your tummy rises and falls with your breath. Continue to just be with your breathing for a while, breathing in all the rich oxygen into your lungs, allowing it to carry on around your body, and maybe as you continue to breathe in all the good, life-giving oxygen, you can just visualise yourself expanding with your breath, and then relaxing as you breathe out. Just notice this cycle, in breath and out breath, expansion and relaxing, for a time. You might be aware of your body resting on the seat on which you're supported. As you continue to breathe, you can draw your gaze inwards now, to your very centre. And as you focus on that place at the centre of your being, you can ask your subconscious to work with you on this exercise. Just listen now, and notice any signs that your unconscious has said yes, it will work with you on this exercise.

Now as you sit here, relaxed, safe, in touch with your centre and your unconscious, ask your unconscious to represent to you your path in life. You can just visualise your path when your unconscious is ready. Notice what the path looks like. Can you see a lot of it, or a little? What is your point of view? Are you on the path already, or are you seeing it from elsewhere?

If you are not yet on the path, I wonder if you can just visualise yourself stepping on to the path, and then see what the path looks like from that part of you which is on the path. Just notice what you can see, if there are any sounds, whether there are any sensations. Take the time now to fully appreciate what it is to fully be on your path in life. You don't need to feel any judgement; just notice how it is.

Now, as you stand on the path, I'd like you to take a moment to look forwards, towards where the path leads to. Really take a moment to see what's in front of you on the path. Maybe it looks like it will be a fairly easy journey. Maybe it is a path which you will need extra help to tread.

As you contemplate your path ahead of you, take a moment and just ask your unconscious, 'what do I need to be able to walk this path fully?' You not consciously come up with an answer, or you may know immediately what it is that you need on this path. As you ask yourself what tools or resources can help you to be on your own path, ask your unconscious to represent them to you. Visualise the resource or resources that you need appearing in front of you or maybe in your hands, in whatever form is right for you. Notice as you look at them, what shape and weight the resources are. Thank your unconscious for bringing them to your attention. It doesn't matter if you don't know what they are or what they're for – it is enough that they are there, in your unconscious whenever you need them.

Now, standing on the path, noticing the path itself and the resources in your own hands, take a step forwards. Notice how the path feels underneath your feet, whether there is any sound as you see your foot coming down on the path in front of you. Be really aware of how it is for you to walk on this path, this path which is yours.

As you walk down the path now, notice whether you are happy with your path. Is there anything which you would like to be different? Visualise the path changing to represent how you would like it to be. How has it changed? Is the path the same? What about its surroundings? Is there anything new? Does it look different? Feel different? Has the sound changed?

Notice now, once again, the resources which you have with you. Are they still OK, or do you need new ones? Visualise placing any resources which you do not need onto the old path, behind you. Now ask your unconscious to provide you with all the resources which you need to walk the new path, the path as you would like it to be. Visualise them, noticing the colours, size, weight, whether they make any sound. Hold on to these resources.

As you walk with your own resources on your path, notice what you see. Look around you, in front of you, being really aware of what your path is, what it is like. How is it to be you on your own chosen path? Is it different to how you normally feel? What are the sensations? Are you hearing anything, from the path, the surroundings, your self?

Take what you've noticed, along with your resources, and place it all into an energy ball in your hands in front of you. Notice how this ball is full of the different images from your path, your surroundings and your own resources. Notice the colours. Notice how it feels – does it vibrate, can you feel the energy, is there any weight to it? Is it making any noise?

Holding this energy ball in your hands, bring it slowly towards you and place it in your self, into your being. Just place it in there, for safe-keeping. Now that you have placed your knowledge of your own path, and the resources you need, you can access this at any time you may need it. Breathe into this part of you where you have stored this knowledge, allowing now any visualisation to just fade away in front of you. Notice the sounds getting fainter and disappearing, the sensations dissolving as you start to notice your breathing once again. Remember you can always get them back whenever you need to.

Spend a few moments now just focussing on that breathing, the steady, life-giving rise and fall of your tummy as you breathe in and out, in and out.

And you can start to bring your awareness slowly back to your body now, noticing any sensations where your body meets the seat underneath you, or the ground. Noticing your feet, your calves, your thighs, your pelvis, your abdomen and lower back, your chest, your shoulders, your internal organs, your arms, your neck and your head. Listening now for any sounds outside of you, noticing them maybe if you hadn't noticed them before.

And if you like you might want to start to bring some movement back, wiggling your fingers and your toes, taking a stretch if you feel like it, or maybe just shifting your weight a little, having a little shuffle in your seat.

And when you're ready you can start to think about opening your eyes, allowing the light in through your eyelids, maybe squeezing them tightly shut before fully opening them, becoming aware of the things which you can see where you are in the room. And just allow yourself to take as long as you like to come round now, ready to go back to your day refreshed and invigorated.

✧ Notice your internal monologue. Sit down with a pen and paper for five minutes. During this time, notice all the things which you say to yourself – all of the thoughts which go through your brain. Write them down on paper. Don't worry, I know this can be uncomfortable, and you don't have to show them to anybody – you can tear them up or burn them straight after this exercise if you like – just write your thoughts down for five minutes. When the five minutes is up, go back to what you have written and examine it critically. What sorts of things do you tell yourself? Is it true? Is there anything you're adding or omitting, any distortion? What is the purpose of doing this? Are you really gaining from not being honest with yourself? Edit your thoughts so that they are more honest. Are they very different? Is this difference distressing? Empowering? Can you find a way to live with yourself with this honesty? Try to notice your tendency to be untruthful with yourself, and when you catch yourself doing it, stop and substitute honesty. Notice whether this causes any great change in your life.

✪ When you are used to the above exercise you can adapt it to your external stories as well. Notice the things that you say to people. Again, write them down if necessary. Now go through the things you said. Are they true? What would happen if you were to tell the truth in this dialogue? What would stay the same; what would be different? Think about it. If it is a situation in which direct truth would be unwelcome to someone, can you think of a way to be honest without being hurtful? As you think about these things, notice what you are saying, and if you find yourself speaking something that is not a truth, find a way to change it.

✪ If you are looking for a way to truly, honestly be, try narrating your current experience or actions in your head, or see them as a written story, but take out the adjectives and remove any 'because' narration, however attached to it you may be. Narrating in this way can sometimes help you to notice your own state and actions – how you are being and what you are doing. When we can see ourselves honestly we can accept ourselves as we are, honestly.

✪ If you are doing your work as best you can, but are finding it hard to focus your attention, you can do something about that. Picture the things which are taking up your attention in front of you. Notice those things in front of you in your mind's eye. Then, taking a deep breath in, reach up and pluck that picture out of the air. As you breath out, move your arm to the side of you, and imagine that you are putting the picture on a shelf. Put it down gently – you might need it later – and surely. Now let it go. You can come back to the things that that picture represents whenever you like, it's waiting for you on the shelf, and now your field of vision is free to focus your attention fully on your work at this moment.

☼ Take note of whether your actions match your values. Often they will, and sometimes they won't, which can lead to conflict in our way of being. At the end of the day sit down with a pen and paper and list all of the actions which you have done today. Then think of your values – what's important to you? Values can be anything and change from person to person, and generally you will know when something is or is not in line with your values. Go through your list of actions. Has anything clashed with your values? If the answer is yes, try to think of a way to handle the same or similar situations in the future in a way which is within your value system. You'll find yourself much happier for this.

☼ **Self acceptance plus Reiki meditation**

For this meditation, as always, get yourself comfortable, sitting or lying on the ground or on a chair. Try to have your spine straight and your body supported, especially your feet and buttocks, and your hips, which support your spine.

Breathe deeply into your centre. Feel the rise and fall of your abdomen as you breathe easily in and out, bringing a sense of relaxation and comfort in with the breath, releasing any worries or tension as you let go. For the next few minutes you're going to be spending some time thinking about yourself, and you can relax into this state as you know that by spending this time with yourself now, you will be able to live more honestly as you create meaning in your life.

So just let yourself breathe for a moment, imagining that as you breathe in, the breath rises from your base to your crown, and as you breathe out, it travels back down your body, starting at the crown and ending at your base. Just let yourself slip into this pattern, breathing in from the feet to the crown, and out down from the crown to the feet, noticing how you relax as you do so.

And now take your awareness to your left foot, noticing how it feels resting on the floor beneath you, noticing any weight or pressure where it rests, becoming really aware of the shape of it, its physical shape, any energy within it, whether that is moving or still, being aware of the makeup of your foot, the skin, the flesh, the veins and lymph, the muscles and bones.

Now bring your attention to your left shin, and become really aware of this. What is it resting on? What is its shape? How does it feel? How is the energy? Notice the skin, flesh, blood, bones and muscles. Notice how they relate to each other.

Now move your attention on again to your left thigh. How is the skin here? The flesh? The muscles and bones, the flow of energy and of blood. Just allow your left thigh to rest in its own shape.

Bring your attention now to your right foot. Again, notice how it feels, resting, notice its position and shape, its physical makeup, skin, bones, muscles, flesh, blood, any energy that is flowing or stationary within the foot.

Now bring your attention to encompass your right calf, noticing the shape it makes, the way it rests, being aware of all the different components that make your calf a calf – skin, bone, muscle, flesh, blood, lymph tissues. It's all there.

Now shift your awareness to your right thigh, again noticing its shape, positioning, how it is supported, how the muscles are, the presence of the bone, the blood, the lymph, the surface of the skin.

And from there you can bring your awareness to your hips and pelvis, noticing how that whole area feels, all of the little muscles, supported by the structure of the bone, the flow of blood, the skin surface and the flesh, noticing if there is any energy that you're aware of there and what that feels like.

And now you can become aware of your abdomen, your lower back, tummy, your internal organs, all of the organs, the kidneys, intestines, your spine, flesh, muscles, and the skin that contains them all.

And now you can move your attention to your upper torso, to the ribs, the muscles, noticing how your shape changes slightly as you breathe, being aware of your lungs and your heart, all of the internal organs which are contained by your ribs, the muscles, the skin. Notice any energy and what it is doing.

Now you can bring your attention down to your left hand, to notice the fingers, the bones, the muscle, the flesh, the way it they rest where you're resting them.

And you can move your awareness to your left arm, noticing the way it hangs from your shoulder, the bend at the elbow, the skin, containing the muscles, the bones, any energy which is flowing or stationary there.

And you can bring your attention over now and back down to your right hand, to the fingers, the shape of the hand, its physical makeup, and how it joins at the wrist to the arm.

Notice the arm, its shape, its position in space and in relation to the rest of your body, the physicalities – the skin, the flesh, the shape of the muscles, the strong supporting bones, the energies.

And now you can bring your attention to your neck, the way it rises from your torso, the way it conducts your breath down into your body, the feel of it, the shape, the position, the flesh, the spine, any energy which might be present.

And your awareness moves to your head, to the weight of it, noticing your face at the front, your ears on the side, being really aware of your brain inside your head and all those wonderful sensory organs contained inside the skull and the skin around it. Notice any energy that is present.

Now expand your attention so that you can be aware of your whole body, from your head all the way down to your toes, and everything in between. This is your body. This is the shape you are.

Now take your breath and your attention down to your abdomen, breathing in deeply, becoming really aware of your centre. And as you relax, you can ask yourself, if I was a colour, what colour would I be? Just imagine that colour now, or maybe it is a mix of colours, just imagine yourself, this unique and special person that is you, here, now, expressed as a colour. And you can flood your body with that colour, that expression of who you are. How does that feel?

And you might feel ready now, to ask yourself, in simplicity and honesty, who am I? Ask yourself that question now, and listen for the answer, watch as it rises within you, feel the certainty of who you are. It may come as an image or series of images, or as sound, or sensations. Just let it come; that's you.

And as you know now who you are, you can take that knowledge, and just draw it in to your very centre, in your abdomen, behind your navel. Just picture that knowledge now of who you are, in the very centre of your being, and feel it there.

And as you feel it there, place your hands on your abdomen and start to send yourself some Reiki, flooding healing, love, and acceptance to yourself, as you are truly.

You can send yourself Reiki for a few minutes now, just allowing that love, healing, and unconditional acceptance take shape within you as the energy surrounds you.

(After as long as you need): And now, you can take your hands from your abdomen, allowing the flow of Reiki to subside, and bringing your attention away from your abdomen as you breathe.

And as you breathe in, you can once again allow yourself to imagine the breath rising up from your toes to your crown, and as you breathe out, from your crown to your toes. As you feel this breath, notice whether you're ready to start to come back to your surroundings now, feeling refreshed and revitalised, alert and at ease with yourself. Feel whether your limbs want to stretch or wiggle, whether you want to shift in your seat or even stand up. Notice any sounds which are coming from outside. When you feel ready, open your eyes, and allow the light of the outside world mingle with that light which is within you. When you are ready, you can get up and go about your day, bringing with you this acceptance of your true self.

✿ If you can find a moment before you start your work, whatever that may be, use Reiki to help you to prepare yourself. Simply sit or stand upright, fold your hands together or in your lap, and start to breathe Reiki in to yourself, with the intention that it enter you, surround you, stay with you and support you in achieving your upcoming task. Spend five minutes or more doing this to help to prepare yourself for your work.

Hito ni shinsetsu ni

Be kind towards people - be compassionate – be kind to others – be kind to every living thing – be compassionate towards yourself and others – be kind to people

Interpretations

This final precept is all about kindness and compassion, and any addendums to this tend only to direct this kindness and compassion either inwards or outwards. We all already have compassion to some degree, and if you're reading this book then the chances are that you experience feelings of compassion, on which you may or may not be able to act, regularly.

So let's take a look at what compassion is about. The word itself refers to a co-passion – or shared feeling – more than to simple feelings of sympathy towards the object of your compassion. This state of shared feeling is not always as easy to reach all the time. However it does embody a sense of understanding, which along with the sympathy which we normally associate with the word compassion, can make powerful changes to your world and the world of those you share it with.

So this precept is about gaining a feeling for people, an understanding of their feelings, hopes, desires and other passions, an understanding of what it is like to be them, as well as a sympathy for their feelings and needs.

But compassion is not simply something to be used with or on other people. Just as important as being kind to others, is the edict to be kind to one's self. It is important to practice kindness and understanding towards oneself, to forgive ourselves the mistakes we make and accept our selves and our thoughts, actions and emotions.

Without this attitude of kindness to ourselves, how can we be kind to others?

There is also a connotation of generosity in compassion and kindness. Whether this means the ability to share material objects, time or skills, or simply acting in recognition of one's own or another's needs, it is important to take the time to be generous, to think further than a purely personal perspective. In generosity lies abundance.

One of the best forms of loving kindness which you as a Reiki practitioner have at your disposal is the ability to send Reiki energy. Sending Reiki in itself is not only an act of loving kindness, but requires that we think of the recipient without judgement, and wish them only well-being. This is why Reiki is so powerful not only for the recipient, but also for the practitioner.

Exercises

- ☼ Practice self-healing, and practice it regularly. You probably already have a method of self-healing. It doesn't really matter too much whether you are moving your hands through a series of hand positions or just breathing the Reiki in to yourself. The important thing is to cultivate a practice of sending yourself self-healing on a regular basis. You may find that if you practice this every day, you will soon achieve some great results in the way you feel and your general wellbeing.

- ☼ Give Reiki. As Reiki is one of the best forms of loving kindness, it is good to give it whenever we are able, to whoever will accept it. You may already treat many people, or you may just be starting out, and not have begun treating other people yet. If you don't already share Reiki with others, offer treatments to your family, friends and acquaintances. You might think that they might not want to know or understand what Reiki is, but you will find that more people are willing to give it a go than not. You can also give distant Reiki – using the distant healing symbol and any distant healing technique you have learned, or if you have not yet learned this, simply focussing on the recipient and pointing your hands in their direction.

✿ Think of a situation with another person, where you may not find it easy to feel compassion. Picture that scene in front of you, at least arm's length away. Watch yourself interacting with the other person; watch what they say and do. Watch the you in the picture. Is that you showing signs of compassion, or something else? How does this manifest in their expression, physiology, posture, gestures? Imagine that you are directing a film, and get the you in the picture to change these things in order to come across as more compassionate.

Now focus your attention on the other person in the scene. Step into that part of the scene where you can see them. Step inside them. Adopt their physiology, expression, gestures, posture. How does that feel? Is there anything there you hadn't really been aware of? What does this person need from the you that is interacting with them?

Now step out of that person, and away from the scene again. Look at the you in the scene. Direct the film so that, retaining the more compassionate expression, posture, gestures and physiology, that you in the scene is able to express compassion towards the other person, showing them kindness and understanding. What needs to happen? Watch yourself doing whatever needs to be done in a spirit of compassion.

Now freeze the scene, and go and step back into it – this time, into the you that you have just been watching behave compassionately. Adopt the physiology, the gestures, the posture and the facial expression. How is that? Does it feel nice? Act out the compassion towards the other person.

Now step back out of the scene, and look at it. Have you got everything you need to act more compassionately? If the answer is not yes, picture yourself having the resources that you need to be compassionate. Add them to the picture, step back in, feel them, act them. Then step back out again.

You can let the scene go now, and think of a time in the future when you might be able to use this compassion. Can you imagine yourself doing so now that you know how to? That's good.

☼ **Loving Kindness Meditation with Reiki**

The loving kindness meditation is found in some Buddhist practice, and involves sending feelings of loving kindness to a series of people, starting with yourself, and moving on through people you know, don't know, and have varying feelings about. I have adapted it here so that instead of feelings of loving kindness you are actually sending Reiki, which is both a cause and an effect of loving kindness.

The meditation: Sit yourself comfortably upright on a chair or on the ground. Take a moment to check you're supported, your breathing is steady, and that you are focussed. You may wish to close your eyes.

Connect to Reiki in the way in which you normally do. Once you have this connection, for the moment just allow the Reiki to flow into the centre of your being, building there, growing stronger.

When the Reiki has built up for a moment, picture a mirror image of yourself sitting just in front of you. Without too much thought, take the Reiki that is flowing in through you, and send it to that image of yourself in front of you. You may wish to move your hands; you may be able to send it using simply your mind. The important thing is to send the Reiki to yourself, in an open, judgement-free spirit of loving kindness. Allow this Reiki to flow for a few minutes, knowing that as you send it to this mirror image of yourself, so it reaches you, connecting you with yourself in love and kindness.

After a few minutes, allow the image of yourself to fade, retaining your connection to the Reiki. Now picture sitting in front of you a loved one or friend, someone whom you already like and care about. As before, send the Reiki to this image of them, using your hands or maybe just using your mind. Send with the intention that this Reiki will reach them only for their well-being. Allow the Reiki to flow for a time.

Again, you can now let the image of this loved one to fade, retaining the connection to Reiki within yourself. Now picture sitting in front of you someone whom you feel fairly neutral about. It could be someone who you know slightly, but do not feel anything towards – you just know who they are. When you have this picture in front of you, once again, send Reiki to them. Remember that the intention is only that

Reiki will reach them for their highest healing good, and suspend all judgement.

After a few minutes, let this image fade or disappear. Now picture someone whom you dislike. It might be someone you know well, or a public figure. You might feel any negative emotion or emotions towards them. Picture them sitting in front of you now. Then, when you are ready, send Reiki to them. To do this, you will have to put aside any negative emotions, and send kindness and wishes for their wellbeing only. Allow the Reiki to flow to them for a few minutes.

Now let this image too fade, and now imagine all of those people – yourself, your loved one, the person you feel neutral towards and the person whom you dislike – imagine them all sitting in front of you together. Take your Reiki and send it to them, with the intention that it is for their wellbeing, and that it reach them all, in equal measure. Allow this to flow for a few minutes.

When you have done this for a few minutes, you can allow the image to fade, and you can disconnect from the Reiki energies in whatever way that you normally do. Stand up, have a walk around, rub your hands together or shake them; do what you need to do to step back from the exercise now that it is complete. This is not always an easy exercise, and can bring about great changes in the way you feel, as well as help bring about wellbeing for those people to whom you have sent the Reiki.

☼ Think of an act of kindness which you can easily do for someone else – someone you know or a stranger, someone who can live without it or someone who is really in need. It is important here to question your motives and your spirit – although you may be acting on the strength of the suggestion in this exercise, you must also approach in a spirit of compassionate understanding – the object here is that your act will really make a difference to your recipient, and any good feelings which you may get from it are irrelevant, so make sure that you have understood their needs and are not acting from what you think they might or should need. Have you got it? Good, go and do it.

✿ One of the most generous things that you can give to somebody is your time. There are probably many causes, situations and people which already evoke in you a feeling of compassion. Be generous with this compassion and give your time and full attention to it – commit to being involved on a regular basis. Again, it is really important here that you act from a point of view of compassionate understanding, and not simply for your own gratification, so if you do make a time commitment to another person or group, you must keep it.

✿ Try to gain rapport with other people, so that you can come to a better understanding of them, which will automatically lead to a more compassionate outlook. One of the best ways to understand how another person is feeling is to try out their physical posture, expression, and movements. If you do this for a while, you will start to understand how they feel. Focus on your similarities with the people you meet – whether you have some of the same experiences, or values, or are doing the same thing. This will help to improve understanding.

✿ Make sure you take time to look after yourself. This might mean taking a break, whether it be for an afternoon or a week, where you can focus solely on your own needs. Look to your physical needs first – are you eating properly, getting enough sleep, exercising? Do you meditate regularly? Maybe it's a while since you received any Reiki, or you could do with a massage. Make time to do all of these things. What do you do for leisure? Would you like to sit and read a good novel, or go walking, or go out for a meal? Maybe you need time for yourself or with friends? Again, make time to ensure that you are meeting these needs. It's not selfish; it's self-care, and we must do these things for ourselves if we are to be any use at all at all of the other loving, giving, things which we do with our lives.

✿ Facilitate someone else's taking a break. Maybe you know someone who could do with some of the things mentioned in the previous exercise. Is there anything you can do to help – offer to help out with a task or responsibility so that they can have this time, or simply invite them to spend time with you doing something nice together? Do it now if it is within your means.

✿ With each person that you come into contact with, ask yourself, 'what does this person need from me?' If you are able to give what this person needs, do so.

✿ Write a letter. A letter is a gift of yourself and your time, and can send joy and hope to another person. Maybe you could write to someone you know, or someone you have lost contact with. It could be someone who needs support, or even someone who is in detention, for whatever reason. In starting a correspondence you create a compassionate understanding with this other person, and a hand-written letter is so unusual these days that it is bound to bring joy to the recipient.

☼ Be mindfully aware of someone you spend time with today. You can practice this with a loved one, family member, colleague or even with a stranger on the bus. They do not need to know that you are doing it. The aim of the exercise is to be more understanding of the people you meet in your life. You may be surprised at what you learn about even the people that you know well. By being present in your relationships as they are now, you let go of your preconceptions, which exist only inside your head, about the people who you deal with, and so you become more present. You may be surprised at what you learn about people's current experience and the compassion which you cultivate as a result.

Observe the way that your subject sits, stands, or positions their body. If you can, notice their breathing rhythms. Focus all of your attention on that person - your experience of this person is what you are living in this moment.

Now reposition your body to match their posture. If you think that this might cause embarrassment, you can modify your positioning so that it does not look mocking. But it's amazing how similar you can make your posture. Slow down or speed up your breathing to match theirs. How does it feel to be in this posture, breathing like this? You may find that you already have a lot of insight into how that other person is today.

Now close your eyes and picture the scene from outside. See yourself in relation to the other person, and notice where they are in relation to you. Studying the scene from outside, notice what is happening here. Be aware of the scene as it is, letting go of any thoughts or judgements about what is going on. What do the people in the scene need? What do you think they are feeling? Is there anything which needs to be done?

Now step into the scene, but instead of stepping into your own skin, step into that of the other person. Look at yourself and what is going on around you. What is it like to be that other person? Do they need anything from you?

Step out of the other person, and back into yourself, bringing your new insights with you. This is a great exercise for becoming more aware of all types of relationships – from the family member who we see so often that we forget to look at them properly, to the difficult colleague or the stranger in the street. By connecting with the people we are with, we connect with the reality of our today.

About the Author

Keziah Gibbons is a Reiki Master and Teacher, a Master Practitioner of the Reiki Drum Technique, and a Master Practitioner of NLP. She brings her training and experience in these disciplines, as well as the attitudes and capabilities which she has learned on her own travels, to the exercises in this book.

For Keziah, healing is a calling, with Reiki at the core of her practice. The application of the Reiki principles, together with meditation and self-healing, has empowered her at all levels of her own life, and she lives to share this empowerment with others, to apply wherever they need it. To learn more about Keziah's work, including treatments, courses and workshops, visit www.vibrantselfhealing.com

Guided Meditations

Many of the meditations and techniques in this book are also available as guided mp3 audios. To find out more, go to www.vibrantselfhealing.com